THE EARLY RIVER VALLEY CIVILIZATIONS

THE FIRST HUMANS AND EARLY CIVILIZATIONS

THE EARLY RIVER VALLEY CIVILIZATIONS

Rebecca Kraft Rector

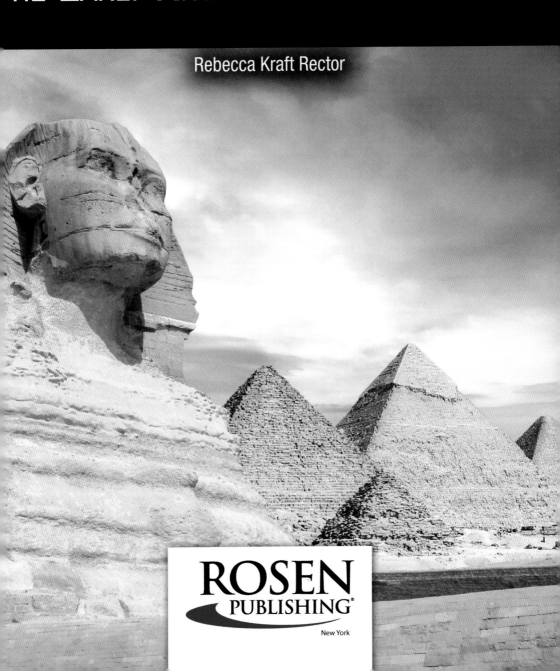

ROSEN
PUBLISHING®

New York

Published in 2017 by The Rosen Publishing Group, Inc.
29 East 21st Street, New York, NY 10010

First Edition

Library of Congress Cataloging-in-Publication Data

Names: Rector, Rebecca Kraft, author.
Title: The Early River Valley Civilizations / Rebecca Kraft Rector.
Description: First edition. | New York, NY : Rosen Publishing Group, 2017. |
  Series: The First Humans and Early Civilization | Includes bibliographical
  references and index. | Audience: Grades 7-12.
Identifiers: LCCN 2015049229| ISBN 9781499463286 (library bound) | ISBN
  9781499463262 (pbk.) | ISBN 9781499463279 (6-pack)
Subjects: LCSH: Civilization, Ancient—Juvenile literature. | History,
  Ancient—Juvenile literature.
Classification: LCC CB311 .R42 2016 | DDC 930.1—dc23
LC record available at http://lccn.loc.gov/2015049229

Manufactured in China

Contents

INTRODUCTION

I n 1826, a traveler in India came across brick ruins. He thought he had found the ruins of an old castle. He wrote about his discovery in 1842, but no one considered it important. In 1856, British engineers building the East Indian Railway found the same ruins and took away some of the bricks to build their railroad bed. It was not until 1920 that archaeologists began investigating the ruins. They dug through the piles of bricks and unearthed the remains of the huge city of Harappa. Evidence showed that it dated from about 2500 BCE. They had found the first signs of the ancient civilization of the Indus Valley.

Archaeological discoveries provide information about ancient civilizations. Archaeology is the science that studies human life in the past by searching for, and analyzing, the remains of cultures. Archaeologists sift through sand and dirt, descend into tombs, comb through garbage pits, and reconstruct pieces of objects. They study pottery, tools, tombs, and writings to form conclusions about the way people lived.

Most of the discoveries about the ancient river valley civilizations did not happen until the 1800s. People are still making important discoveries about these civilizations today. We now know that the first civilizations developed in different parts of the world around the fourth century BCE. Each civilization rose in the valleys along major rivers. Rivers provided water and were a source of rich earth. Rivers were also a

The ruins of the Indus River valley city of Harappa revealed that the city was well-planned, with straight streets and a fortress on one end.

means of transportation. There were disadvantages to settling in river valleys, however. Rivers flooded, there were no natural protective barriers in a valley, and there were usually limited natural resources.

The first civilization to develop was Mesopotamia, located between the Tigris and Euphrates Rivers in the region that is the modern country of Iraq. Mesopotamia was in southwest Asia. The next civilization arose on a different continent. In northeast Africa, the ancient Egyptians lived on a narrow strip of land beside the Nile River. They had little contact with other early civilizations. The Harappan civilization of the Indus River valley emerged next, in an area that is now Pakistan and northern India. Archaeologists have found evidence that the Harappan civilization carried on extensive trading with the Sumerians of Mesopotamia. The Indus River valley is in Asia, as was the last of the four great civilizations. The Yellow River (Huang He) valley people in China were isolated from other civilizations and developed a unique culture.

These four civilizations are called the cradles of civilization because they built the first cities, created the first forms of permanent writing, and developed many other inventions that are still used today. These civilizations were the foundation for the societies that came after them.

CHAPTER 1
THE RISE OF EARLY RIVER VALLEY CIVILIZATIONS

For much of human history, people spent their lives roaming in small groups. They needed to keep moving and searching for food. They hunted, fished, and gathered plants. Around 10,000 BCE people started learning how to farm. This period is called the Neolithic Revolution. It was a revolution because it changed human life completely. People no longer needed to roam the land, hunting and gathering food. The ability to grow their own food allowed people to stay in one place. They were able to plant crops and domesticate animals. It was a significant step toward civilization.

DEVELOPMENT OF EARLY RIVER CIVILIZATIONS

The earliest civilizations developed along rivers in climates that were mostly hot and dry. They were surrounded by deserts, which offered some protection from enemies. The rivers provided water for the crops. The flooding of the rivers left behind silt that

LEARNING TO FARM

Early humans hunted wild animals and gathered wild plants to keep from starving. They had to move around without settling in one place. When they learned to gather seeds, sow them in rich soil, and harvest the plants, they no longer had to search for food. They settled in one place and tended the land. People invented plows to help loosen the soil for planting. Wheat, barley, and peas were some of the first crops.

They also learned to domesticate animals such as cattle, goats, and sheep. Animals were another source of food and material for clothing. Animals also helped lighten the workload, as when oxen pulled the plows.

Both crops and animals need water to survive. Rivers provided water as well as rich soil after flooding. Learning to control the floodwater through irrigation techniques was one of the first needs of the people in early river valley civilizations. Once the floodwaters were tamed, farming began on a large scale.

enriched the land. Silt is the sand and soil carried by moving water. The river constantly replenished the land with new minerals and rich soil.

However, the floods also destroyed crops and homes until people learned to build ditches to control the waters. People gathered together to dig and maintain the ditches and canals. They were able to

These ancient Egyptians are irrigating their crops by using a simple mechanism called a shadoof to lift water from the Nile River.

cultivate large areas of crops and produce ample amounts of food.

With a reliable source of abundant food, people were able to do more than just survive. They lived peacefully with each other, built permanent structures, and learned skills that were important for their communities. By living together, people were better protected and could trade goods to fill their needs. However, larger groups of people created large amounts of waste, and people needed to be organized for the good of the community. As populations increased, their societies became more complex. The societies developed into civilizations.

CHARACTERISTICS OF EARLY RIVER VALLEY CIVILIZATIONS

All civilizations have characteristics in common, including the
early river valley civilizations. The
main features of a civilization
are cities, governments,
social classes, specialized
jobs, art, monuments,
and written language. The
people are also united by
a common belief system.
Cities or large pop-
ulation centers are one
of the characteristics of

*These are the ruins of the
ancient Mesopotamian city of
Uruk, which was one of the
world's first cities.*

any civilization. As more and more people settled together, the first cities in the world formed. Some cities were
planned, such as those of the Indus River valley civilization, but many grew up from smaller settlements.
Some had houses that were raised above floodwaters
on platforms. Others were built on higher ground or on
the ruins of old buildings.

Another characteristic of civilization is a government.
Once the early river valley civilizations formed cities,

governments were needed to direct the people in projects that helped everyone, such as maintaining canals. When the civilization expanded through exploration or wars, the government administered those lands as well. The government was usually headed by a king, but, in earlier times, a priest might be in charge of managing the community.

When farmers produced enough food to support many people, some people stopped farming and gained new skills that were useful to the civilization. Specialized jobs are another characteristic of a civilization. These include merchants, doctors, scribes, and architects. Merchants who bartered or traded their goods with other cities or countries were called traders. Trading with other countries spread ideas and culture. Successful traders could gain wealth for themselves and their families.

A difference in wealth created a social hierarchy, meaning that some people were richer, more powerful, and more important than others. Social hierarchies can also be based on the kind of work a person performs. Social hierarchies are another characteristic shared by civilizations. In the early river valley civilizations, kings and nobles ranked at the top of the social structure, with poor people and slaves at the bottom. Usually it was difficult or impossible for people to change their ranks. However, the ancient Egyptians allowed people to rise based on their own merit.

Although people within the ancient river valley civilizations were divided by their social status, they came together in another way. Each civilization had a belief system, or religion, that was common to all the people. None of the early river valley civilizations practiced the same religion. However, religion was an important part of each civilization. Religion told people how to live their lives and what would happen after they died. It shaped their culture, including their daily lives and traditions. Their religion united them, and those strong beliefs could lead to war against those who did not have the same belief system. Priests were important in most ancient civilizations because they instructed the people about what the gods wanted them to do.

The Egyptian god of wisdom, Thoth, has the head of an ibis in this 4,000-year-old painting on papyrus. The Egyptians believed in many gods.

A written language is another characteristic of civilizations. It allows governments to keep records of taxes, laws, and many other administrative items. Each civilization was able to record its history and create literature for others to read. All of the early river valley civilizations used symbols to represent sounds and words. However, archaeologists have found it difficult to read the ancient writings. The Egyptian hieroglyphs were not translated until 1822, after the Rosetta Stone was discovered. Scholars are still not able to read the writing of the Indus Valley civilization.

THE BRONZE AGE

Early humans made tools and weapons out of stone. Archaeologists call this period the Stone Age. When humans began using metal, they moved into the Bronze Age. The early river valley civilizations developed into Bronze Age civilizations. Later they learned to work with iron and moved into the Iron Age.

Bronze is a mix of copper and tin that is melted together. Bronze is hard and can be shaped into different forms. It can be melted and poured into molds and then hardened. It was used for tools and weapons. Archaeologists have found bronze daggers, swords, helmets, chisels, hammers, and nails. Bronze was also used for artwork and jewelry.

Civilizations also create art and architecture, especially monuments to honor important rulers. Monuments also help people remember their civilization. Mesopotamian ziggurats and Egyptian pyramids are examples of monuments. Art of the river valley civilizations includes pottery, statues, jewelry, tomb paintings, and bronze-work.

The ancient peoples developed skills in mathematics and sciences to help them in their lives. Mathematics helped them measure fields and build monuments, and it was also important when trading goods. Ancient people developed a knowledge of astronomy as they studied the skies to create a calendar that they could use predict the beginning and end of the growing season, as well as annual floods.

Tool making was also important. The early river valley civilizations advanced from stone tools to bronze ones. They invented the wheel, sail, plow, drill, and many other items that are still important today.

CHAPTER 2
MESOPOTAMIA, THE CRADLE OF CIVILIZATION

Ancient Mesopotamia was located between two rivers, the Tigris and the Euphrates. In fact, "Mesopotamia" means "land between the rivers." Today, most of ancient Mesopotamia is located in the country of Iraq.

Mesopotamia made up a large part of the Fertile Crescent. The Fertile Crescent is a region shaped like a half circle that includes the eastern Mediterranean and the northern part of the Nile River, in Egypt.

GEOGRAPHY

Surrounding Mesopotamia were the Syrian Desert to the west and the Arabian Desert to the south. The Zagros Mountains were to the east and the Taurus Mountains to the north. The Tigris and Euphrates meet and empty into the Persian Gulf in the southeast.

Rain fell mostly in the north. Summers were hot, and winters were colder. The rain in the north was plentiful enough to grow crops. Farther south, rainfall could not support the crops.

When the Tigris and the Euphrates flooded, the rivers brought silt onto the land. Silt was left behind when the waters retreated, building a flat, fertile area for farming.

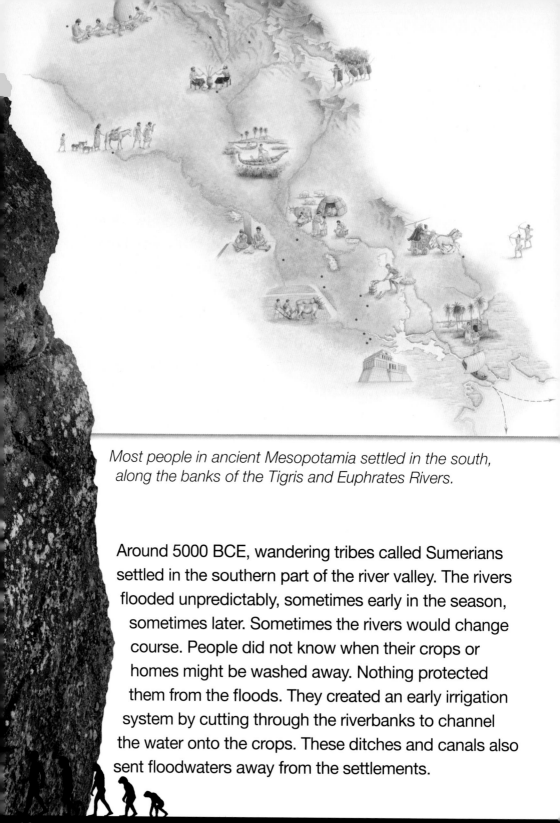

Most people in ancient Mesopotamia settled in the south, along the banks of the Tigris and Euphrates Rivers.

Around 5000 BCE, wandering tribes called Sumerians settled in the southern part of the river valley. The rivers flooded unpredictably, sometimes early in the season, sometimes later. Sometimes the rivers would change course. People did not know when their crops or homes might be washed away. Nothing protected them from the floods. They created an early irrigation system by cutting through the riverbanks to channel the water onto the crops. These ditches and canals also sent floodwaters away from the settlements.

Sumerians in the southern marshy areas reclaimed land by putting reed mats in the marshes there. They built mud brick walls to protect themselves from floods and enemies.

CITIES

Around 4000 BCE, the Sumerians built the world's first cities. The people may have gathered together to build cities for protection. Possibly the cities were built so that people could work together to dig irrigation ditches.

The first city was Eridu. Other cities were Ur, Uruk, Nippur, Lagash, and Kish. The early cities were surrounded by land and were called city-states. They shared the same culture, but each one had its own government.

By about 2300 BCE, Mesopotamia was controlled by the Akkadian Empire, the capital of which was the city of Akkad. Around 1900 BCE, the Amorites conquered all of Mesopotamia, and Babylon became the capital. It was such a powerful and important city that the region was called Babylonia. By 600 BCE, Babylon had a population of 200,000 and was circled by defensive walls for ten miles (sixteen kilometers) around.

POLITICAL LEADERS

The gods were always at the top of any hierarchy in Mesopotamia. Ancient Sumerians believed that all land

belonged to the gods. Priests were responsible for the offerings, sacrifices, and rituals meant to please the gods. Priests
were also overseers of the land and were in charge of the first
cities. They directed groups of people to take care of crops or
to dig irrigation ditches. They also made important decisions
about war, trade, and commerce.

Around 2400 BCE, new rulers emerged from the warlords
who were constantly battling for control of the fertile river
valleys. It was believed these kings received their power from
the gods and passed this power to their family members.

*Ancient Sumerians brought offerings to the ziggurat, or holy
mountain. This modern drawing shows an artist's idea of
what the Ziggurat of Ur looked like.*

The priests maintained control of religion but recognized the authority of the kings over political issues. The kings had officials to carry out the details of government, such as taxes, construction, and settling disagreements.

THE SOCIAL ORDER

A person's role in life placed him or her at a certain level in society. This social hierarchy was connected to how much money and influence the person had. In the early city-states, a priest was in charge, organizing the farmers to tend the crops and provide food for all. Once there was enough food, people could do specialized tasks, such as becoming craftsmen, laborers, or merchants. This created the roles of a social structure.

Later, kings took control and became the top of the hierarchy, followed by priests. The king and priests were wealthy and their wealth was increased with taxes and offerings. Noblemen and officials were next, followed by people who owned land. Merchants rose in status if they became wealthy through trade. The poorest were the farmers, laborers, and craftsmen. Slaves on the bottom of the hierarchy had neither power nor wealth.

People's daily lives were affected by how wealthy they were and what they did in society. Early Sumerians lived in huts made from reeds. Later, the homes

MERCHANTS AND TRADE

Early merchants traded among villages, using boats as the main method of travel. Later, carts were drawn by mules and oxen. Sumerian pottery was a highly prized item. Other merchandise included copper ore and surplus grain. Sumerian bronze work, especially armor and weapons, was valuable.

Sumerians traded with at least one other river valley civilization, the Harappans of the Indus valley. Small disks called Harappan seals have been found in Mesopotamian ruins. By 1700 BCE, trade included dates, grain, lapis lazuli, wood, fish, and horses. Merchants traveled together in caravans for protection against thieves. Merchants also used camel trains to move goods in and out of Babylon.

were made from mud bricks with reed roofs. The poor had tiny, single-story homes. The rich had two-story, multiroom homes, often with a central courtyard.

Farmers grew wheat, barley, and peas. They raised cows, sheep, pigs, goats, ducks, and geese. Some people caught fish, but the poor rarely ate meat. They had bread and soups of boiled barley and wheat. They also had vegetables and fruits, such as garlic, onions, dates, and figs. The rich had banquets with meat and beer. Honey and fig syrup sweetened the food. Food was stored in reed baskets or in chests made of baked clay.

The roles of men and women mostly remained the same over the years. In ancient Sumer, women brewed the beer and wove cloth. Both men and women wore tunics or long draped garments of wool or linen. Men arranged marriages and were the heads of the household. They took care of business and religious tasks. Typically, women married young and had no role other than daughter, wife, and mother. They cooked, cleaned, and looked after the children. Women had to be obedient to husbands or fathers. Marriages were arranged and dowries were given to the new husband to support his wife. Divorces could be granted if a husband abused his wife. Only upper-class women could own land and have an income.

CULTURE

Mesopotamian art included carvings, murals, sculpture, and pottery. Pottery was especially important in the early Ubaid period, when it was an important trade good.

Archaeologists have discovered evidence of musical instruments including flutes, lyres, drums, rattles, and harps. Sheet music has also been discovered.

Mesopotamians developed new forms of architecture, including the arch and column. They also used domes. They built temples and ziggurats for worship.

Ziggurats were temples placed atop pyramid-shaped structures. Steps on the outside led to the temple.

Between 3100 to 2000 BCE, the Sumerians developed the first writing system. Called cuneiform, it consisted of symbols pressed into clay tablets. Later Mesopotamian people used the same system. Having a method of writing enabled them to

This ancient Sumerian clay tablet from around 2360 BCE used cuneiform writing to record a count of goats and rams.

record business transactions, laws, history, prayers, and stories. Mesopotamia had the world's first library.

Ancient Mesopotamians created literature such as myths, epics, and legends, including the *Epic of Gilgamesh*. *Gilgamesh* is thought to be the oldest written story.

RELIGION

The ancient Mesopotamians were polytheistic, meaning they worshiped many gods. Each city-state had its own god, and the god was believed to own the lands.

This statue was discovered in a temple dedicated to Abu, the god of vegetation. It is thought to be of Abu's wife.

Kings and queens were believed to be representatives of the gods or even gods themselves.

Religion was a constant presence in everyday life. Religion explained how people could lead a good life, and it explained what happened after death. It shaped the social order and how people treated one another. People who had the same beliefs felt connected to each other. These strong beliefs could lead to war with people of different beliefs.

People worshiped in temples and at shrines in their homes. They provided offerings and paid taxes to support the temples. The priests sacrificed animals to the gods. They also did charity work. High-status women could become priestesses.

SCIENCE AND TECHNOLOGY

The Sumerians invented channels to direct river water into the fields and away from their homes. This single invention let them grow plenty of food, which allowed large groups of people to live together in cities.

The Sumerians studied the sun, the moon, and the stars, probably as part of their religion. The Babylonians continued this study and made advances in astronomy. They created a calendar and clocks. The Babylonians also built on the basic Sumerian arithmetic and created more advanced systems of mathematics. They were the first to have the concept of zero.

The Sumerians are believed to have invented the wheel around 3500 BCE. They developed metalworking techniques in bronze and copper. They also invented a seed plow, which could cut through the soil and drop seeds at the same time. They created sails for their boats, allowing them to move more quickly on the rivers.

CHAPTER 3

ANCIENT EGYPT, THE GIFT OF THE NILE

The ancient Egyptian civilization grew up from settlements along the Nile River. It lasted for about 3,000 years, from around 3100 BCE to 30 BCE. The civilization began when Narmer, also called Menes, unified Upper and Lower Egypt. This created the first major nation-state. Narmer also established the first dynasty.

There were three main time periods, called the Old Kingdom (2686 BCE to 2181 BCE), the Middle Kingdom (2055 BCE to 1650 BCE), and the New Kingdom (1550 BCE to 1069 BCE). After the fall of the New Kingdom, Egypt eventually became part of the Roman Empire.

GEOGRAPHY

The Nile River valley is in Egypt, in northeastern Africa. The Nile flows from south to north, and Upper Egypt is to the south and Lower Egypt is in the north. The valley is surrounded by desert to the west, south, and east. To the north is the Mediterranean Sea, with a narrow land bridge to the northeast. The area makes up the western part of the Fertile Crescent.

The Nile River flooded at fairly predictable times. People planted in the rich mud left behind. They dug channels to direct river water into ponds for irrigating the fields. They also used shadoofs if the river was low. Shadoofs are devices used to lift water. The Egyptians built their homes on high ground and on top of the ruins of old buildings.

CITIES

Unlike Mesopotamia, Egypt had few cities. People spread out along the banks of the Nile to farm the land. They did not need cities for protection because the surrounding deserts and the Mediterranean Sea helped keep them safe from enemies.

This map of ancient Egypt shows the ancient capitals of Memphis, Amarna, and Thebes along the Nile River.

Around 2900 BCE, Memphis became the first capital city. The capital moved over the years. Other Egyptian capitals included Thebes and Akhetaten, also known as Amarna.

Archaeologists have found the stone foundations of some towns. The towns were surrounded by walls. Drainage channels ran down the middle of them. The streets were straight and narrow, with separate areas for the rich, the craftsmen, and the poor. There was no sewage system. People threw their waste into the river, into pits, or into the streets.

POLITICAL LEADERS

The pharaohs of ancient Egypt ruled over everything. The pharaoh was thought to speak to the gods and sometimes to be a god himself. The pharaoh was the head of the government, armies, agriculture, and religion. He

appointed a grand vizier to help administer the government, as well as local governors and officials. There were several government departments, including ones for treasury, judiciary, army, and agriculture. Everyone paid taxes, including

This is a statue of pharaoh Khafre, who ruled during the fourth dynasty (about 2575 BCE–2465 BCE).

peasants and farmers. There were taxes on property, produce, livestock, income, imports, and exports.

A legal system allowed everyone—rich and poor, men and women—to argue his or her case before a panel of judges. The king decided only the most important cases. Many high-ranking officials were relatives of the pharaoh or other nobles. However, men of lesser rank were allowed to move into powerful positions.

When the pharaohs were weak, the central government also weakened. Around 1630 BCE, between the Middle Kingdom and the New Kingdom, the government was weak, and the Hykos conquered Lower Egypt. They ruled for about a hundred years until they were forced out and the New Kingdom began.

Strong and influential pharaohs included Djoser (2691 BCE to 2625 BCE), Thutmose III (1479 BCE to 1426 BCE), and Ramses II (1279 BCE to 1213 BCE).

THE SOCIAL ORDER

The social hierarchy of ancient Egypt depended on wealth and position. The pharaoh was at the top, with his officials, high priests, and nobles below him. Next came skilled men such as doctors and scribes, followed by craftsmen, soldiers, farmers, and tomb builders. Slaves had no status and were at the bottom of the hierarchy. The structure was somewhat flexible.

A man of low rank could rise to a higher position through his own merit. Wealth could be gained through trade and commerce. The Nile was the main transportation route for trade with other lands. Traders brought in minerals, oils, spices, and horses. They exported cereal crops, dried fish, and papyrus.

Farmers grew wheat and barley to make breads, cakes, and beer. Some of the vegetables they grew included beans, lentils, peas, onions, and radishes. Fruits such as grapes, melons, and dates were also cultivated. The Egyptians raised

This tomb painting from around 1419 to 1380 BCE shows workers picking grapes and treading on them to make wine. Wine containers are shown in the center.

cows, goats, sheep, pigs, ducks, and geese. Fish could be caught from the Nile River. Poor people ate little meat, but the wealthier people ate different kinds of meats, spices, fruits, and vegetables.

Flax was grown and woven into linen clothes. Clothing was usually white, but some wealthy people had it colored with plant and mineral dyes. Men wore kilts or skirts, and women wore long, straight dresses. Babies and young children did not wear clothing. Both men and women wore jewelry, makeup, and perfume.

Houses were made from mud bricks, with thick walls to keep out the heat. Most Egyptians lived in homes with small windows and straw matting on the floors. In cities and towns, houses were built tall and narrow. They could be four stories high. The pharaoh lived in a pal-ace. Wealthy people had large houses with as many as seventy rooms.

Women and men were equal under the law, and women could own property. Most women married, had children, and took care of their homes. They could farm and run businesses, make perfume, work in a court or temple, or become priestesses. Five women even became pharaohs. Men farmed or held jobs.

There were a number of different jobs in ancient Egypt. Many people were farmers. Unskilled workers were servants or made beer, bricks, and linen. Boys were apprenticed into trades. Higher-ranking boys went to school. After school, they became scribes, government officials, or priests. Skilled workers also included architects, doctors, and dentists.

CULTURE

Ancient Egyptian artists and craftsmen were highly skilled. They created paintings, sculpture, pottery, and jewelry. Tombs, temples, and palaces held the majority of the art pieces. The hot, dry climate has preserved many of these creations.

Music and dance played a large part in religion and festivals. Dancers and musicians also worked as entertainers

The Great Pyramid at Giza is the tomb of the pharaoh Khufu. The two large pyramids next to it are the tombs of his son and grandson.

for the wealthy. They played flutes, lyres, drums, rattles, harps, and wind instruments. Often women and slaves were musicians.

Ancient Egyptians used a written language as early as 3500 BCE, when hieroglyphs were carved into clay tablets. Hiero-glyphics used pictures and symbols to stand for words and sounds. Around 3000 BCE, the ancient Egyptians learned to make paper from a reed called papyrus. They wrote with brushes and ink and simplified the hieroglyphs into a curved style called hieratic. Around 650 BCE, hieratic was simplified even more into a style called demotic.

THE ROSETTA STONE

Archaeologists were not able to read hieroglyphs for many years. The key to understanding hieroglyphic writ-ing was the Rosetta Stone, which was discovered in 1799. This huge slab of stone was carved with writing in three languages, including hieroglyphic, demotic, and Greek. Scholars thought the languages probably all said the same thing. The Greek was translated by 1803, but it was not until 1822 that Jean-Francois Champollion de-coded the hieroglyphs.

The Rosetta Stone was written around 196 BCE when Ptolemy V became pharaoh. It told of his generosity and his many good deeds.

Much of ancient Egyptian literature was written to guide the dead in the afterlife. Spells, prayers, and songs were written on tomb walls or buried with the dead. During the New Kingdom, the spells were written on papyrus scrolls and placed into coffins. These scrolls came to be known as the *Book of the Dead*.

The ancient Egyptians are famous for their architectural monuments built of stone. They built palaces, tombs, obelisks, and temples. But it is the pyramids of the Old Kingdom that are the most impressive. The Great Pyramid of Giza, built around 2550 BCE as a tomb for the pharaoh Khufu, is 481 feet (147 meters) high and probably weighs 6.5 million tons.

RELIGION

Like the people of Mesopotamia, the ancient Egyptians were polytheistic. There were more than 2,000 Egyptian gods. The gods represented every part of life. One of the most important gods was the sun god, Ra or Re. Each city had its own special god, and when that city gained in importance, so did the god. Pharaohs were considered to be divine.

People worshiped at home at their shrines. Only priests and priestesses worshiped in the temples. In addition to prayers and sacrifices, worship included festivals and feasts.

Ancestors were worshiped, and people believed in a life after death. Rulers were buried in tombs with everything they would need for the next life. This included jewels, food, servants, and animals. Their bodies were preserved as mummies, and their tombs were hidden within huge pyramids to keep them safe from thieves.

SCIENCE AND TECHNOLOGY

The Egyptians made copper, bronze, and iron tools. They were the first to build huge monuments with stone. Their skill with mathematics helped them design huge pyramids. Mathematics and astronomy played a part in developing a calendar with 365 days in a year. Ancient Egyptians invented a paper made of papyrus. They also made advances in medicine.

The Hyksos invaders brought new technology to Egypt, including new weapons, horses, and chariots. They also had new techniques for weaving and working with bronze.

CHAPTER 4

INDUS VALLEY, THE CRADLE OF INDIAN CIVILIZATION

T he Indus valley civilization is also known as the Harappan civilization or Sindhu-Sarasvati civilization. This civilization was larger in area than Mesopotamia and Egypt. It lasted from 3300 to 1700 BCE before it declined. It was once thought that Aryan invaders moved into the area in 1500 BCE. However, scholars now believe that the Aryan civilization, now called the Vedic culture, grew out of the existing Harappan culture.

The Indus Valley civilization was unknown until it was rediscovered in the 1920s. Excavation of the sites is ongoing and archaeological remains have been found over 1.5 million square miles (3,885,000 square km). Much remains to be learned about the civilization.

GEOGRAPHY

Most of the Indus Valley is located in the country now known as Pakistan. Parts of it stretch into India and Afghanistan as well. The Indus River is the longest river in Pakistan. It begins in the Himalayas and empties into the Arabian Sea. The Sarasvati River once joined it before it reached the sea. However, the Sarasvati dried up and no longer exists. The Indus River valley is in the southern part of the river, near the Arabian Sea. The Indian Ocean is to the south, the Himalayas are to the north, Afghanistan to the west, and India to the east.

Snowmelt in spring and monsoons in summer caused the Indus to flood on a regular basis. Flooding added silt to the land and created a fertile flood plain. The Harappan people controlled floodwaters through irrigation. They dug trenches from the riverbanks and directed the water toward their crops and away from their homes. They also built defensive walls against the floods. There were no rocks in the valley so the walls were built from clay bricks. The walls were about 5 feet (1.5 m) wide. The Harappans also built on top of platforms to avoid floods. Some platforms were almost 40 feet (12 m) high.

CITIES

The Harappans were the first to plan their cities rather than letting them grow at random. The two largest cities, Mohenjo-daro and Harappa, were built in the same way. Each of the cities was about one square mile (2.5 square km) and thoughtfully planned and constructed. Streets were laid out in straight lines. Cities had neighborhoods of people who worked at the same jobs, such as merchants and craftsmen. The cities had granaries, kilns, and wells. There was indoor plumbing, and drains and pipes carried waste out of city. This was probably the world's first city sanitation system.

The Great Bath in Mohenjo-daro was brick-lined with steps leading down to it. A courtyard with columns surrounded it.

The Great Bath in Mohenjo-daro was in the middle of the city and may have been a public bath. Some people believe it may have been used for religious ceremonies. It was 39 feet (12 m) by 22 feet (7 m) in size.

More than a thousand cities have been found, but none of the others were as large as Harappa and Mohenjo-daro. The coastal city of Lothal had a docking facility for trading ships.

POLITICAL LEADERS

The political structure of the Harappan civilization is not known. It does not seem that one city had control over the others. There is no evidence of rulers, although the organization and planned structure of the cities indicates there was some kind of government. The Harappan civilization appears to have been a peaceful one. There were no known battles or conflicts. It is assumed that the Harappans bargained or made agreements instead of war. Few weapons have been found in archaeological sites, and there are no signs of violence on skeletal remains.

This seal dates from about 2000 BCE. It shows a horned cow, or possibly a unicorn. Both the seal, made of a stone called steatite, and the impression it makes are shown here.

The Harappans are known to have traded with other early civilizations such as Persia and Mesopotamia. Harappan artifacts, such as seals, have been discovered in Mesopotamia. Seals are small rectangles, often made of baked clay or a soft stone called steatite, or soapstone. They usually had a picture carved on them. Often the pictures were of animals. Sometimes there was writing as well. Some seals had holes in them. A piece of twine could have been threaded through the hole so the seal could be worn around the neck or tied around a container. Archaeologists think that the Harappans used these

SEAL ANIMALS

Archaeologists have found thousands of the flat stone rectangles known as seals. The seals were probably used by Harappan traders to identify goods. They have been found throughout the Indus valley, as well as in Mesopotamia and other regions. The seals usually had writing and an animal carved on them. The animals included bulls, elephants, and rhinoceroses.

The most common animal on seals resembles a unicorn. The animal has the body of a bull and the head of a horse with a horn on its head. Some people think the unicorn simply looks like a cow. This animal may have represented the Harappan government or an important Harappan family.

seals to label their pots and baskets. They may have shown ownership, a destination, or even whether taxes had been paid.

The Harappans transported goods by using boats on the river, as well as by seagoing craft. Traders walked through mountains and forests, sometimes with carts pulled by bulls. They also used pack animals such as camels and elephants. The traders probably traveled in groups for protection against thieves and wild animals.

The large area of the Indus valley civilization contained many resources, unlike Egypt or Mesopotamia. The Harappan civilization exported gold, copper, jewelry, pottery, grain, and cloth. They imported silver, lead, copper, and jade. They seem not to have used money. Instead they probably used a barter system.

THE SOCIAL ORDER

The extensive trading and the fertile land made the Harappan people prosperous. Most of the people lived well and the differences in living between the rich and poor may not have been as pronounced as in other civilizations.

In contrast, the Vedic people had a social hierarchy with people at different levels called castes. Brahmin priests were at the highest social level. Rulers and warriors were in another caste, farmers were in another, and servants and laborers were members of the lowest caste.

Harappan farmers grew wheat, barley, fruit, and vegetables such as beans and chickpeas. They were one of the first civilizations to grow rice and sesame, and the first to raise chickens. They also raised cows, sheep, goats, and pigs. They ate beef, goat, and mutton. The cows and goats provided milk and butter, while the chickens produced eggs.

Houses were similar within the cities, with no large differences between rich and poor. The houses were built of baked mud bricks with thick walls. Most houses were at least two stories high and many had water and drains. Larger houses were built around courtyards. Windows with wooden bars across them faced the courtyards. People may have slept on the flat roofs to keep cool in the summer.

The Harappans were among the first to grow cotton and spin it into thread. Although it is not certain what kind of clothing they wore, it was most

This street view in the city of Mohenjo-daro shows the walls made of baked mud bricks.

likely made from cotton. Probably rich people wore a finer type of cotton and more elaborate clothing. Both men and women wore jewelry. Ancient cave paintings show people in loincloths, saris, and turbans. It is possible that the Harappans continued to dress in this manner. Small clay figures show women wearing short skirts, which is another possible indicator of the way that women dressed.

Culture

Harappan art included painted pottery and seals. Harappan craftsmen also produced toys and jewelry made of beads, precious stones, ivory, and seashells. Small sculptures have been discovered, but it is possible they were brought in from a different country. Drums, tambourines, and stringed instruments have been found by archaeologists. Music and dancing were probably popular.

Like other river valley civilizations, the Harappans developed a writing system. Pictograph writing has been found on pottery and seals, some dating from 3500 BCE. Unfortunately, the writing cannot be read because no one has been able to decipher the script.

The writing could give information about the civilization and its people. Until it is decoded, little can be known of Harappan religion, politics, society, and government. More is known about the later Vedic civilization because it used the Sanskrit language.

Archaeologists excavated this sandstone statuette in Mohenjo-daro and named it "the Priest King."

RELIGION

Most scholars believe Harappans were polytheistic, meaning they worshiped many gods. Small female statues have been found, which may mean they worshiped a mother goddess. Harappans probably believed in an afterlife since they included tools and food when they buried their dead.

The Vedic culture incorporated some Harappan beliefs, and over time the religion developed into Hinduism. The Vedic people cremated their dead and believed in reincarnation.

SCIENCE AND TECHNOLOGY

The people of the Indus civilization were among the first to have a uniform system for measuring and weighing things. This made it possible to precisely engineer their irrigation systems, flood walls, wells, drains, and roads. They invented bronze tools like the circular saw, drills, and needles.

CHAPTER 5
YELLOW RIVER, THE CRADLE OF CHINESE CIVILIZATION

The Yellow River civilization is also known as the Huang He civilization. "Huang He" is the Chinese name for the Yellow River. The Yellow River is the second longest river in China (the Yangtze is the longest).

Periods in Chinese history are named after the ruling families, or dynasties, of the time. The oldest Yellow River dynasty, beginning around 2000 BCE, may have been the Xia dynasty. Most scholars think that it is a mythical dynasty, mentioned in stories but with no archaeological evidence of its existence. In 1959, archaeologists discovered a city in the Henan Province that some believe is an ancient Xia capital. However, many scholars remain unconvinced.

Much evidence exists for the Shang dynasty, which followed the Xia. However, the dates of the dynasty are debated. Evidence indicates the Shang ruled from about 1600 BCE to about 1040 BCE. The later part of the Shang dynasty is sometimes called the Yin dynasty. It was conquered by the Zhou dynasty, which lasted until about 256 BCE.

This Shang dynasty horse-drawn chariot was excavated in the Yin ruins. Yin, an ancient Shang capital, is the site of many archaeological finds.

GEOGRAPHY

The Yellow River civilization formed in the northern part of China, along the Yellow River in the North China Plain. The river starts in the Plateau of Tibet, flows through the Loess Plateau, and empties into the Yellow Sea. The area was isolated, with the Pacific Ocean to the east, desert and the high Plateau of Tibet to the west, the Gobi Desert to the north, and the Himalaya mountain range stretching across the southwest. The weather in the north was cool, without much rain, and winters could be severe.

The Yellow River got its name from the yellow-brown loess, or silt, it carried in its waters. The large amount of loess in the water caused the river to flood periodically. When it flooded, the river left loess behind and built up fertile soil. The floods, however, could be so devastating that the river was called "China's Sorrow."

Legend says that Emperor Yu of the Xia dynasty built the first system of dikes and drainage channels to control the Yellow River. Later, the Zhou built canals and dammed the river to irrigate the crops.

CITIES

The Yellow River dynasties had many different capital cities. One of the earliest, around 1700 BCE, was Zhengzhou. Another was the early Shang capital, Anyang, which was rediscovered in the late 1800s. Ruins of the last capital city of the Shang, Yin, were found nearby. Luoyang was one of the capitals of the Zhou dynasty.

Shang cities were large and had many parts. Excavations of the city of Yin show that the city included a palace, different housing areas for workers, and workshops for casting bronze. It had royal ancestral shrines, an area for royal tombs, and a sacrificial pit. Yin had a ditch around it to help keep out floodwaters.

Most cities had walls to keep out invaders. The Shang dynasty city of Zhengzhou had huge defensive walls 60 feet (18 m) wide and 30 feet (9 m) high.

POLITICAL LEADERS

Legend says that Emperor Yu ruled during the Xia dynasty. In 1523 BCE, Tang became the first king of the Shang dynasty. His power was passed down through his family. During the Shang dynasty, the king was the religious head as well as the political ruler. He ruled over everything, announced when it was time to plant crops, and made all the laws. He appointed nobles to rule local areas. These nobles paid tribute to the king and provided him with soldiers and laborers. Priests helped the king in his religious duties and advised him by trying to predict the future. Warriors were important because there was constant warfare. They had bronze weapons and chariots. Skilled craftsmen ranked above the peasants, who worked the land or did other labor with tools of stone or bone.

In 1027 BCE, Wu Wang defeated the Shang dynasty and created the Zhou dynasty. The political structure of the Zhou dynasty was much like that of the Shang. However, it had a feudal system of government. The king gave nobles power over their own areas, and these lords agreed to be loyal to him. The lords still had to pay the king tribute and provide warriors and laborers. Many of the lords also worked as officials in the king's government.

THE SOCIAL ORDER

Social hierarchies were tied to the political hierarchies. Those who had wealth and power ranked

A Shang dynasty craftsman carved this jade tiger more than three thousand years ago.

above others. The king, nobles, priests, and warriors were at the top of the social structure. Craftsmen and peasants were below them.

Traders traveled between cities with bronze work and jade. Ancient China was isolated, and there was no trade with other civilizations. Trading between cities increased during the Zhou dynasty, and a merchant class developed at the same rank as skilled craftsmen.

Rulers and nobles lived in palaces, with many rooms, several courtyards, and high roofs. The buildings were made of timber over earth foundations that had been rammed hard by pounding. Sometimes the palaces were built on platforms to avoid floodwaters. Wealthy craftsmen had houses, often with two rooms and a window. Poorer craftsmen and peasants lived in pit houses, which were dug partially underground.

Farmers grew wheat, barley, rice, and millet. They raised sheep, pigs, cattle, dogs, horses, and oxen. People hunted for meat and also ate fish and shellfish.

The wealthy had silk clothing, which was sometimes dyed. The poor wore cotton. Both men and women wore jackets, closed with sashes, over skirts. Men farmed, hunted, and fished. They were usually in charge of their families, and families with sons had a higher status. Poor people might kill female babies if they did not have the resources to feed them. Children had a duty to respect and obey their parents. If they did not, they were severely punished and could be killed. A woman's job was to have sons, cook, and look after her family. Women were also in charge of weaving silk, which was a complicated process.

CULTURE

Art of the Shang and Zhou dynasties included glazed and carved pottery. Craftsmen worked in bone, jade, ceramics, stone, wood, shells, and bronze. Many kinds of bronze objects were created and decorated. One of the largest bronze containers discovered by archaeologists weighed almost 2,000 pounds (900 kg). It was probably used in a religious ceremony. Music and dance were important parts of religious rituals. Bells, chimes, drums, stringed instruments, and flutes have been recovered.

The Shang dynasty had a form of pictographic writing, which was an early form of modern Chinese writing. The spoken language was somewhat similar to the modern Chinese language. The first books were prob-

The writing on oracle bones like this one provides information about rulers, beliefs, and social life. More than 150,000 oracle bones have been discovered.

ably made of bamboo or silk during the Shang dynasty. A series of documents have been found that are said to be from the early Zhou dynasty. Scholars disagree as to whether they were actually written during that time period. The documents include speeches and political debates.

RELIGION

Both the Shang and Zhou people worshiped many gods. The king was believed to be able to communicate directly with the highest god. This gave him great religious power as well as political power. The Zhou king was called the Son of Heaven, reflecting the idea that he had a connection to the god.

People of both dynasties also worshiped their ancestors and believed ancestral spirits communicated with the gods. Offerings and prayers were made at ancestor shrines. If the ancestors were not shown respect, then bad fortune would follow.

The ancient Chinese believed in a life after death. Kings were buried with everything they would need in the next life, including chariots, servants, animals, food, and valuables. Their tombs were enormous and probably needed thousands of workers to complete them. Poor people, however, were buried in pits with no possessions. Sometimes they were simply tossed into unused wells or garbage pits.

ORACLE BONES

Priests sacrificed animals and humans, especially prisoners of war, to please the gods. The shoulder bones of oxen and the shells of turtles were used by priests to try to tell the future. The priest wrote questions on the bones. The bones were then burned with a hot poker until they broke. The priest examined the breaks to find the answers to questions. The bones were called oracle bones. An oracle is someone, or something, that is believed to communicate with the gods. Oracle bones have the earliest evidence of writing in China.

SCIENCE AND TECHNOLOGY

The ancient Chinese knew how to work with bronze, even before the Shang dynasty. Shang craftsmen advanced this technology, learning to cast bronze from molds.

The Shang used both solar and lunar calendars. Each year had 360 days and 12 months. Each month had 30 days.

Late in the Zhou dynasty, around 700 BCE, craftsmen began to work with iron. Around the same time, the concept of crop rotation was introduced. Planting different crops in a field led to fewer diseases and a more fertile ground.

All of the early river valley civilizations have left important legacies for the future. All prospered for hundreds of years and then failed—except China. The only way to learn about them is through the writings and objects they left behind. The Chinese civilization, however, is the world's oldest continuous civilization, existing for more than 7,000 years.

This is a bronze ritual vessel from the Shang dynasty. It is known as the chaj-cha bird.

TIMELINE

c. 9000 BCE Farming begins in Mesopotamia.

c. 4000 BCE The Sumerians begin to build the world's first cities in the river valley between the Tigris and Euphrates Rivers in Mesopotamia.

c. 3500 BCE The wheel is invented in Mesopotamia.

c. 3100 BCE Egyptian civilization begins when Narmer unites Upper and Lower Egypt into one nation-state.

c. 3000 BCE In Mesopotamia, the Sumerians invent the world's first writing system, called cuneiform.

c. 2600 BCE The cities of Harappa and Mohenjo-daro rise in the Indus River valley.

c. 2550 BCE The Egyptians build the Great Pyramid at Giza.

c. 2400 BCE The Mesopotamian ruler Sargon founds the world's first empire, Akkad, after conquering the Sumerians.

c. 2000 BCE Xia, the first, and perhaps legendary, dynasty begins in the Yellow River valley.

c. 1900 BCE The Babylonian Empire begins.

c. 1700 BCE The Harappan civilization of the Indus River valley declines.

c. 1600 BCE The Shang dynasty takes power in the Yellow River valley.

c. 1500 BCE Vedic culture begins in the Indus River valley.

c. 1150 BCE The Zhou dynasty overcomes the Shang in the Yellow River valley.

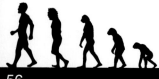

GLOSSARY

archaeologist Someone who studies how people lived in the past by finding and examining remains such as bones and tools.

barter To exchange one thing for another, without using money.

city-state A city, and its surrounding land, that has its own government.

civilization A well-organized society with certain characteristics such as cities, government, and a written language.

cradle of civilization A place where a civilization first began.

crescent A curved shape, usually with thin ends and a thicker middle.

cuneiform Shaped like a wedge; an early system of writing with wedge-shaped characters.

domesticate To tame wild animals or plants so they can live with, and benefit, humans.

dynasty Rulers from one family who are in control for a long time.

fertile Able to produce many plants or offspring.

hierarchy A system in which people are placed at different levels of importance.

hieroglyphics An ancient Egyptian writing system using pictographs.

irrigation A method of providing water to plants and crops, often by ditches or pipes.

merchant Someone who buys, sells, or trades a large quantity of goods.

papyrus A grasslike plant that was used to make a kind of paper.

pictograph A symbol or picture, often used in a form of writing to represent words or sounds.

polytheistic Believing in more than one god.

scribe Someone who can write and make copies of documents.

silt The sand and soil carried in moving water, such as a river.

ziggurat A pyramid-shaped structure with a temple on top.

FOR MORE INFORMATION

The Canadian Society for Mesopotamian Studies
University of Toronto
4 Bancroft Avenue, 4th Floor
Toronto, ON M5S 1C1
Canada
(416) 978-4531
Website: http://projects.chass.utoronto.ca/csms/main.html
This society's purpose is to stimulate interest among the general
   public about Mesopotamia.

Carnegie Museum of Natural History
4400 Forbes Avenue
Pittsburgh, PA 15213
(412) 622-3131
Website: http://www.carnegiemnh.org
This museum's Walton Hall of Ancient Egypt includes antiquities
   related to the themes of cultural evolution and history, nautical
   tradition, social organization, daily life, and funerary religion.

National Museum of Natural History
PO Box 37012
Smithsonian Institution
   Washington, DC 20013
(202) 633-1000
Website: http://www.mnh.si.edu/exhibits/eternal-life
The Eternal Life in Ancient Egypt exhibit explores Egyptian beliefs
   through its burial rituals.

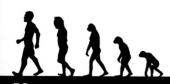

The Oriental Institute
The University of Chicago
1155 E 58th Street
Chicago, IL 60637
(773) 702-9520
Website: https://oi.uchicago.edu/museum-exhibits
This museum has permanent galleries about Egypt and
    Mesopotamia, as well as other ancient peoples.

Royal Ontario Museum
100 Queen's Park
Toronto, ON M5S 2C6
Canada
(416) 586-8000
Website: http://www.rom.on.ca
The Wirth Gallery of the Middle East has artifacts and
    exhibits from the Fertile Crescent.

WEBSITES

Because of the changing nature of Internet links, Rosen
Publishing has developed an online list of websites related
to the subject of this book. This site is updated regularly.
Please use this link to access the list:

http://www.rosenlinks.com/FHEC/river

FOR FURTHER READING

Allan, Tony, and Charles Phillips. *Ancient China's Myths and Beliefs*. New York, NY: Rosen Publishing, 2012.

Boyer, Crispin. *National Geographic Kids: Everything Ancient Egypt*. Washington, DC: National Geographic, 2011.

Bramwell, Neil D. *Discover Ancient China*. Berkeley Heights, NJ: Enslow, 2014.

Brooks, Philip. *The Story of Ancient Civilizations*. New York, NY: Rosen Central, 2011.

Crawford, Harriet E. W. *The Sumerian World*. London, England: Routledge, 2013.

Fullman, Joe. *Ancient Civilizations*. New York, NY: DK Publishing, 2013.

Gibson, Karen Bush. *Ancient Babylon*. Hockessin, DE: Mitchell Lane, 2013.

Martin, Claudia. *The Indus Valley*. London, England: Wayland, 2014.

Nardo, Don. *Daily Life in Ancient Egypt*. Chicago, IL: Heinemann Raintree, 2015.

Sen, Benita, and Yatindra Kumar. *Indus Valley*. Logan, IA: Perfection Learning, 2011.

Van Pelt, Todd, and Rupert Matthews. *Ancient Chinese Civilization*. New York, NY: Rosen Central, 2010.

West, Tracey. *Temple Run: Race Through Time to Unlock Secrets of the Ancient Worlds*. Washington, DC: National Geographic, 2014.

Wood, Alix. *Mummification*. New York, NY: Gareth Stevens, 2014.

Wright, Rita P. *The Ancient Indus: Urbanism, Economy, and Society*. New York, NY: Cambridge University Press, 2010.

BIBLIOGRAPHY

Amstutz, Lisa J., and Elizabeth McGovern. *Ancient Egypt*. Minneapolis, MN: Essential Library, 2015.

Atkins, Marcie Flinchum. *Ancient China*. Minneapolis, MN: Essential Library, 2015.

Bancroft-Hunt, Norman. *Living in Ancient Mesopotamia*. New York, NY: Chelsea House Publishers, 2009.

Carnegie Museum of Natural History. "Life in Ancient Egypt." Retrieved October 29, 2015 (http://www.carnegiemnh.org/online/egypt).

Cunningham, Kevin. *Classical Civilization: India*. Greensboro, NC: Morgan Reynolds Publishing, 2013.

Head, Tom. *Ancient Mesopotamia*. Minneapolis, MN: Essential Library, 2015.

Independence Hall Association. "Ancient Civilizations: China." Retrieved November 2, 2015 (http://www.ushistory.org/civ/9.asp).

Nardo, Don. *Early River Civilizations*. Greensboro, NC: Morgan Reynolds Publishing, 2011.

Rowell, Rebecca. *Ancient India*. Minneapolis, MN: Essential Library, 2015.

UNESCO World Heritage Centre. "Yin Xu." Retrieved December 2, 2015 (http://whc.unesco.org/en/list/1114).

University of Chicago. "Ancient Mesopotamia: This History, Our History." Retrieved October 26, 2015 (http://mesopotamia.lib.uchicago.edu).

Wachtel, Alan. *Chinese of the Shang, Zhou, and Qin Dynasties*. Chicago, IL: World Book, 2009.

Williams, Brian. *Daily Life in the Indus Valley Civilization*. Chicago, IL: Heinemann Raintree, 2015.

INDEX

ABOUT THE AUTHOR

Rebecca Kraft Rector is a writer, librarian, and researcher. She is the author of the Rosen biography *Alan Turing*, as well as the author of novels and more than 100 nonfiction articles. She is more accustomed to digging up facts, rather than artifacts, but one of her novels includes a character who is an archaeologist. Researching this book has inspired her to set a new novel in an ancient river valley civilization.

PHOTO CREDITS

Designer: Matt Cauli; Editor: Amelie von Zumbusch; Photo Researcher: Bruce Donnola

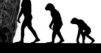